The Diary of Anne Frank

Written by **Jenny Alexander**
Illustrated by **Stewart Lees**

Contents

'Dear Kitty...'	4
The secret annexe	11
Life in hiding	17
Betrayed	24
The diary lives on	28
Time line	30
Anne Frank today	32

'Dear Kitty...'

Anne Frank was born in Germany in 1929, but her family moved to Holland when she was four years old. They were Jewish, so they were not safe in Germany after Hitler came to power. Hitler and his Nazi party had racist beliefs. They hated the Jews.

Anne's parents gave her a diary on her thirteenth birthday. She had never had a diary before.
She pretended it was a friend she could tell all her secrets to. She called it 'Kitty'.

Holland

When Anne started writing her diary, Hitler had invaded Holland and life was beginning to get hard for the Jews in Amsterdam. His plan was to kill all the Jews in Europe.

First, Hitler made a law that Jews were not allowed to mix with non-Jews. To show they were different, they had to wear a yellow star at all times.

This means Jew in Dutch.

Jews were not allowed to:

- Visit non-Jews
- Run their own businesses
- Go shopping, except between 3pm and 5pm
- Go out of doors between 8pm and 6am, even to sit in their own garden
- Ride in trams or cars
- Own a bicycle
- Visit swimming pools or theatres

Then, Hitler sent orders for Jews to go to 'work camps'. Nobody really knew what happened at the work camps, but they knew that people who were sent there never came back.

Anne Frank's father, Otto, was afraid that his family might be sent to a work camp, so he began to prepare a secret hiding-place in an annexe behind his warehouse.

The secret annexe

On July 5th 1942, Anne's older sister Margot got a letter saying she must go to a work camp. The next day, the Frank family moved into the secret annexe.

Although there was very little space in the secret hiding place, Anne's father let four other Jewish people who wanted to hide from the Nazis move in with them.

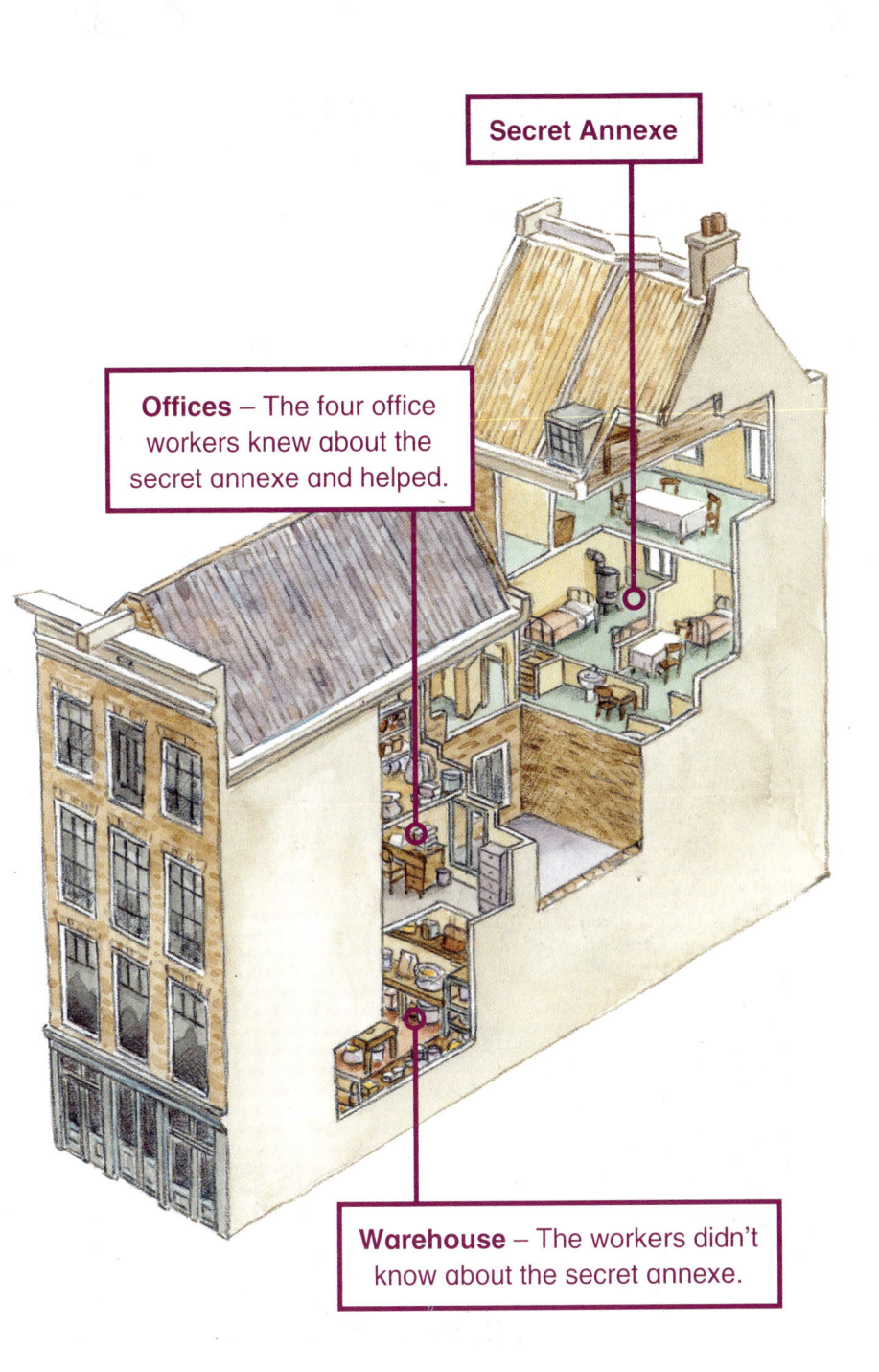

Secret Annexe

Offices – The four office workers knew about the secret annexe and helped.

Warehouse – The workers didn't know about the secret annexe.

The eight people in the secret annexe could not have survived without help. Four Dutch people who worked in the office looked after them. These brave people knew they could be shot by the Nazis if they were caught.

Miep

Johannes

Bep

Victor

One night, thieves broke into the warehouse downstairs. The people in the annexe could hear them moving around. They kept completely still and quiet. They were terrified of being discovered.

After that, Victor, one of the Dutch office workers, built a bookcase in front of the door to the secret hiding place.

'Now our secret annexe has truly become secret...' wrote Anne.
(21st August, 1942)

Life in hiding

Every day, as soon as the warehouse workers arrived, the people in the annexe had to be as quiet as mice. They couldn't move around, or run water or flush the toilet. They could only speak in whispers. Anne and her sister, Margot, spent a lot of their time doing school work and reading.

All the people hiding in the annexe looked forward to Saturdays, because then Miep would bring five new library books for them to share. Three or four times a week, she would also bring them food.

Because Anne could not contact any of her school friends, 'Kitty' became the only one she could talk to.

At night, the Frank family used to go downstairs to the office to listen to the radio. They heard that thousands and thousands of Jews in the work camps were being put to death in gas chambers.

Anne felt very guilty that she was safe in the annexe when so many other Jewish people were being killed.

Anne tried not to feel angry or bitter about the horrible situation she was in. She hardly ever complained. But one Christmas Eve she wrote this:

'I long to ride a bike, dance, whistle, look at the world, feel young and know that I'm free.'
(24th December, 1943)

After more than two years in hiding, the people in the annexe heard on the radio that British and American soldiers had invaded France and the war was nearly over. Anne was full of hope and joy.

'Oh, Kitty... I have the feeling that friends are on the way.'
(6th June, 1944)

23

Betrayed

Anne thought they would all be safe but then, on a beautiful summer morning in August, three Dutch policemen and their Nazi commander marched into the factory offices. Armed with pistols, they stormed up the stairs.

They pulled open the door hidden behind the bookcase. They knew about the secret annexe. Somebody had betrayed the people hiding there. To this day, no one knows who it was.

The men arrested everyone. Anne didn't even have time to grab her precious diary. After they had gone, Miep put Anne's diary in her drawer for safe keeping.

Anne, her parents, her sister and the four other Jews who had hidden in the secret annexe were sent to death camps. Anne's father was the only one who survived.

The diary lives on

When the war was over, Otto Frank returned to Amsterdam. Miep gave him Anne's diary.
Otto wept when he read that Anne's greatest wish was to become a famous writer.

So Otto had Anne's diary published. Since then, millions of people all over the world have heard of Anne Frank and her diary has become one of the most famous books of all time.

Time line

1929 Anne is born, on 12th June.

1933 Hitler comes to power in Germany. Frank family move to Holland.

1940 The German army invades Holland.

1942 Anne is given a diary for her thirteenth birthday. The family goes into hiding.

1944 **June** – British and American soldiers invade France.

1944 **August** – The people in the annexe are arrested and sent to a concentration camp.

1945 **March** – Anne dies in the concentration camp.

1945 **May** – Germany surrenders. British and American soldiers free everyone held in concentration camps.

31

Anne Frank today

- Today people all over the world know about Anne Frank and her diary has been published in many languages.

- If you go to Amsterdam you can visit the annexe where Anne hid for two years. It is a museum now.

- If you can't go to Amsterdam, the Anne Frank Trust UK organises a travelling exhibition that visits towns throughout the UK.

- The Trust organises various celebrations on National Anne Frank Day, which is on 12th June – Anne's birthday. They also organise the Anne Frank Awards for Moral Courage.

- Young people under 16 can join the Young Friends of the Anne Frank Trust UK.

If you want to find out more, visit www.annefrank.org.uk or phone 020 8340 9077.